Hidden Life

What's Living in Your Bedroom?

Andrew Solway

Heinemann
LIBRARY

H **www.heinemann.co.uk/library**
Visit our website to find out more information about **Heinemann Library** books.

To order:
☎ Phone 44 (0) 1865 888066
🖨 Send a fax to 44 (0) 1865 314091
💻 Visit the Heinemann Bookshop at www.heinemann.co.uk/library to browse our catalogue and order online.

First published in Great Britain by Heinemann Library, Halley Court, Jordan Hill, Oxford OX2 8EJ, part of Harcourt Education.
Heinemann is a registered trademark of Harcourt Education Ltd.

© Harcourt Education Ltd 2004
The moral right of the proprietor has been asserted.

Editorial: Nancy Dickmann and Tanvi Rai
Design: David Poole and Paul Myerscough
Illustrations: Geoff Ward
Picture Research: Rebecca Sodergren
Production: Séverine Ribierre

Originated by Dot Gradations
Printed and bound in China by South China Printing Company

The paper used to print this book comes from sustainable resources.

ISBN 0 431 189641
08 07 06 05
10 9 8 7 6 5 4 3 2

British Library Cataloguing in Publication Data

Solway, Andrew
Hidden Life: What's Living in Your Bedroom?
  579.1'7554
A full catalogue record for this book is available from the British Library.

Acknowledgements

The publishers would like to thank the following for permission to reproduce photographs:

Alamy Images p. **4**; Corbis p. **15b** (Kelly Mooney Photography), p. **9** (Tom Stewart); Holt Studio International p. **20t**; Oxford Scientific Films pp. **18**, **23t**; Oxford Scientific Films p. **20b** (Mike Birkhead), p. **23b** (Frank Schneidermeyer); Science Photo Library p. **5t** (R. Maisonneuve, Publiphoto Diffusion), p. **16** (John Burbridge), p. **13r** (A.B. Dowsett), p. **27b** (Eye of Science), p. **24r** (Vaughan Fleming), p. **27t** (Pascal Goetgheluck), p. **25t** (E. Gueho), p. **7b** (Tony and Daphne Hallas), p. **10t** (Andy Harmer) p. **17** (K.H. Kjeldsen) , p. **10b** (Dr Karl Lounatmaa) , pp. **6-7** (Medical Stock Photo), pp. **5b**, **22** (Astrid and Hanns Freider Michler), p. **24b** (Sidney Moulds), p. **8** (Alfred Pasieka), p. **12** (Chris Priest and Mark Clarke), pp. **6b**, **14**, **19** (David Scharf), p. **11** (Lee D. Simon), p. **15t** (Sinclair Stammers), p. **13L** (Linda Steinmark Custom Medical Stock Photo), p. **26** (Andrew Syred); Tudor Photography p. **21**

Cover photograph of bedbugs, reproduced with permission of Science Photo Library/Eye of Science.

Disclaimer

The paper used to print this book comes from sustainable resources.

Contents

Any words appearing in the text in bold, **like this,** are explained in the Glossary.

Many of the photos in this book were taken using a microscope. In the captions you may see a number that tells you how much they have been enlarged. For example, a photo marked '(x200)' is about 200 times bigger than in real life.

Taking a closer look

A bedroom isn't the sort of place you expect to find lots of life. All animals need food, so unless you have regular midnight feasts, there aren't many pickings for pests such as mice and cockroaches. But if you could take a look around your bedroom with a microscope, you might be surprised at what you would find.

A bedroom doesn't contain much of what we would call food, but some tiny creatures eat strange stuff. How would you fancy eating skin flakes instead of cornflakes? Or perhaps you would prefer chewing on your clothes, or gnawing some wood? You might find creatures that eat all these things living in your bedroom.

This bedroom looks empty of all living things. But if you could look closer, you would find lots of hidden life.

Bugs in the bed

Your bed is one place where you can find hidden life. At night it's warm, and there's a very good source of food – you! Another place that tiny bugs like to live is in the carpet. You might also find some in your wardrobe, snacking on old clothes.

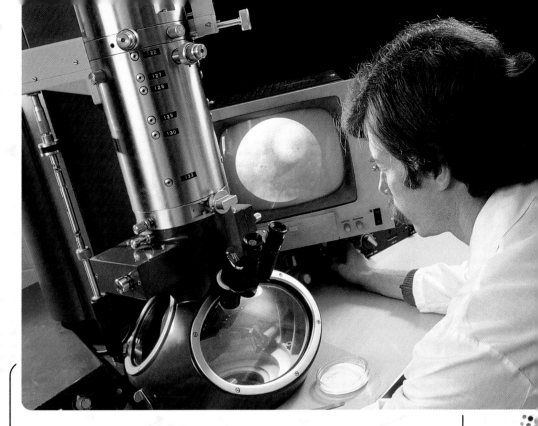

🔍 *Electron microscopes are expensive and complicated to use. To look at creatures under an electron microscope, they have to be killed.*

🔍 *Light microscopes are easy to use, and they can be used to look at living creatures.*

Microbes

Turn up the power on your microscope and you will start to find lots of tiny **microbes** around the bedroom. There are microbes living on your skin, so whenever you touch something you leave some of these microbes behind. There are even microbes floating around among the dust in the air. Every time you breathe in, some of these microbes get into your nose and throat.

MICROSCOPES

The reason we know so much about the hidden life around us is because scientists have studied microbes using microscopes. The kind of microscope that you might have used at school or at home is a light microscope. A powerful one can magnify things up to 1800 times. But to get a close look at really tiny microbes such as **bacteria**, you need an **electron microscope**. This can magnify objects up to half a million times.

Specks of dust

When the sun comes in through your bedroom window, you might see golden specks dancing in the sunbeams. These specks are particles of dust. Under a microscope, a speck of dust becomes a mixture of all kinds of things.

This sample of household dust contains clothing fibres, pet hairs and flakes of human skin.

Pollen grains often have beautiful, elaborate shapes (x1310). Their shape may help them to float on the slightest current of air.

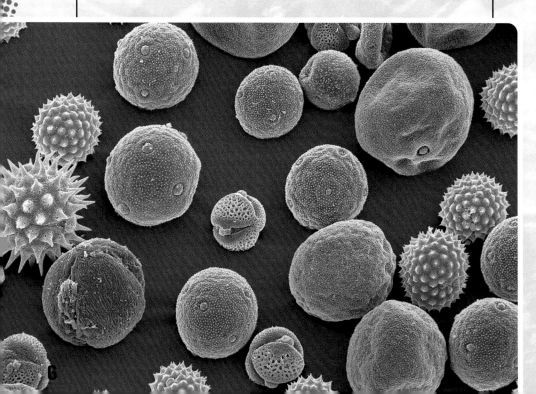

What do you think dust is made of? Bits of rock perhaps, or soil? In fact, it's neither of these things. The most common thing in household dust is skin. The outer layers of our skin are made of dead **cells**. We are constantly shedding tiny bits of this dead skin. New skin grows below the surface to replace the skin we lose.

Dust is so complex a mixture that the dust from a particular place is different from the dust from anywhere else. Forensic scientists (scientists who investigate the scene of a crime) study the many types of dust, and can use this information to connect a criminal to the scene of a crime.

🔊 *These streaks of light in the night sky are meteors – small pieces of rock burning up as they enter the atmosphere. They add to the dust found on Earth.*

An amazing mixture

Household dust is a mixture of an amazing number of things. As well as skin there is hair, fibres from clothing, the droppings of insects and other tiny creatures, and living things such as **pollen** from plants, **bacteria** and other **microbes**.

COSMIC DUST

Some of the dust particles in your house may be visitors from outer space! Every day, large and small rocks from outer space hit the Earth as it travels round the Sun. Most of these rocks break up into tiny dust particles as they fall through the **atmosphere**. About 40,000 tonnes of space dust fall to Earth each year. This is a tiny amount compared to the total amount of dust in the air, but there are probably a few specks mixed in with the other dust in your bedroom.

mattress, your pillows, or the carpet without you ever knowing they are there. But if you suffer from **asthma**, they may be a problem.

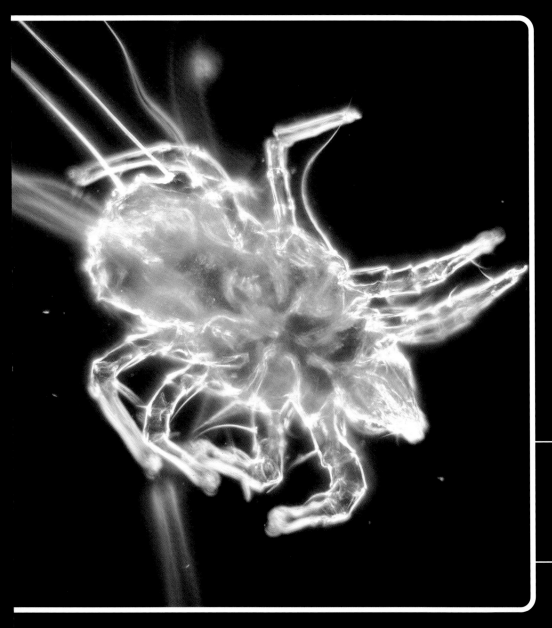

Dust mites are about a fifth of a millimetre long. They have no eyes, but the long hairs on their bodies are sensitive to touch and help them find their way around. Dust mites are **scavengers** that live on whatever food they can find. One of the main things they eat is flakes of skin. They also eat **fungi**, **pollen**, parts of dead insects and other tasty-sounding food!

Dust mites are translucent (partly see-through), which makes them very difficult to see (x188).

Mites in their millions

You won't believe how many dust mites there could be in your bedroom. A pillow may contain thousands of mites, while 10 million mites could be living in your mattress.

The amount of dust in your bedroom will affect the numbers of dust mites. But dust mites like warm, wet conditions, and the conditions in your bedroom are more important than the amount of dust. A house in a warm, wet **climate** will have more mites than a house in a dry, cold place.

How mites live

Dust mites begin life as an egg, which hatches after a few days into a **larva**. The larva eats similar food to adults. Once it reaches a certain size the larva **moults** twice (sheds its skin) passing through two **nymph** stages. After eating and growing for a time it moults again to become an adult.

Adult mites **mate**, and soon after the male dies. The female mites lay 40 to 100 eggs over a period of 2 months.

Mite allergy

Although mites themselves do us no harm, their droppings become part of household dust, and for some people this can be a problem. Many people are **allergic** to dust mite droppings, and this can cause symptoms such as sneezing, red eyes and a runny nose. In some people it can trigger an attack of asthma.

Modern vacuum cleaners now come equipped with filters small enough to capture dust mite droppings. Older models would merely blow clouds of these tiny particles all over the room.

living dust

As we have seen, living things are part of the dust in the air. **Microbes** may float freely in the air, or they may be part of bigger dust particles or droplets of liquid.

Earth star is a type of fungus that grows in woodland. This earth star is releasing a cloud of spores.

When a bacterium forms a spore (red), the **nucleus** of the cell is surrounded by a tough coating with several layers (x57,456).

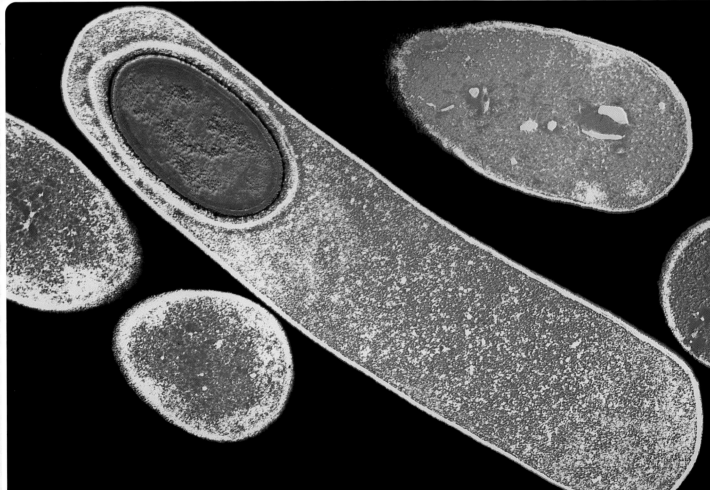

Bacteria

Bacteria are tiny, simple living things, each one just a single **cell**. They are small enough to float in the slightest breeze. However, bacteria dry out quickly in the air, so they have to be protected when they are **airborne**. Some bacteria survive because they are inside tiny water droplets. Others form a thick-coated **spore** when they find themselves in harsh conditions. Inside this spore, the bacterium can survive drying out, low and high temperatures, and harmful chemicals. If and when conditions improve, a new bacterium grows from the spore.

Fungi

Fungi are neither plants nor animals. Most fungi either grow on dead or rotting material, or they are **parasites**.

Fungi reproduce by making spores. These are not like bacterial spores: they are fungal 'seeds'. Each fungus produces millions of very small, light spores (see page 25), and often they are released into the air to spread on the wind.

Viruses

The tiniest living particles in the air are **viruses**. Viruses are made up of an outer layer called the coat and an inner layer of **DNA**. A virus cannot move, eat or reproduce by itself. But if it comes into contact with the right kind of living cell, it infects the cell and uses it to make copies of itself. Some viruses cannot survive outside a living thing for very long, but others can survive for long periods in the air.

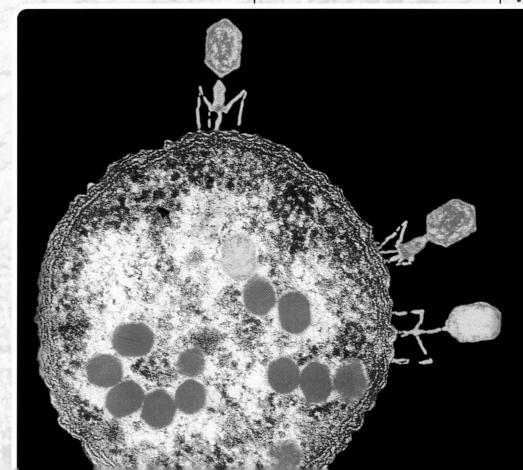

The strange shapes on this Escherichia coli *bacterium are T2 phages – viruses that infect bacterial cells (x138,040).*

Airborne illnesses

At some time you have probably had a few days off school with a bad cold or flu, lying in bed coughing, sneezing and feeling miserable. When you are laid up in bed, always make sure you use a hanky when you cough or sneeze. Otherwise you will be spreading **microbes** around that could infect someone else.

*In many countries babies are **vaccinated** against whooping cough. The vaccine protects them against the disease.*

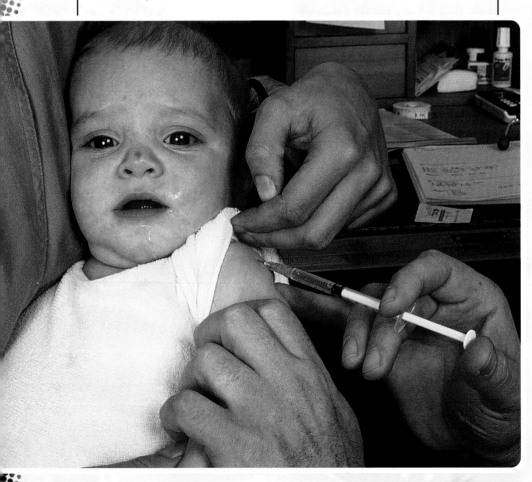

Some microbes in the air can cause disease. Colds, flu, whooping cough and tuberculosis are just some of the diseases caused by **airborne** microbes. These airborne diseases are often passed on by coughing and sneezing.

How airborne diseases spread

When you cough or sneeze, millions of tiny liquid droplets shoot out of your nose or mouth. If you have a cold, flu or other airborne disease, some of the droplets will contain disease microbes. If someone else breathes in some of the droplets, the microbes get into their body and they may get the disease.

Colds and flu

Illnesses such as colds and flu are caused by **viruses**. Colds are caused by a group of very tiny viruses called rhinoviruses that

When you cough and sneeze a cloud of tiny droplets shoots out into the air.

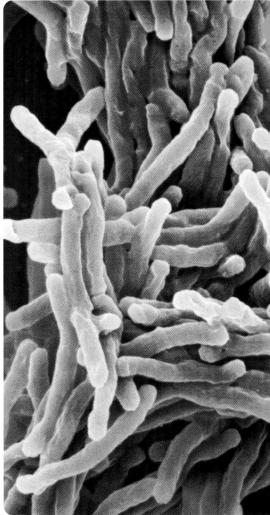

Mycobacterium tuberculosis, the bacteria that cause tuberculosis.

infect the nose (rhinovirus means 'nose virus'). Flu (influenza) viruses are much bigger than rhinoviruses. They attack the nose, throat, and lungs.

We have some cold and flu viruses in the nose and throat most of the time. But if we breathe in a type of cold or flu virus that our body hasn't met before, we get ill. After a time, the body builds up a **resistance** to the new virus, and we recover.

Whooping cough

Whooping cough is a disease caused by a **bacterium** called *Bordetella pertussis*. This tiny bacterium infects the **cells** that line the throat. It causes nasty bouts of coughing that end in a 'whoop' sound as the person struggles breathe in.

TUBERCULOSIS

The most important bacterial disease transmitted through the air is tuberculosis (TB). It is caused by bacteria. TB kills 2 million people in the world every year. It is most common in poor countries, because the disease often affects people who don't get enough good food, or aren't healthy enough to fight off disease.

Bedbugs

The biggest item of food in your bedroom is you!
We have seen already how dust mites live off bits of
skin that you leave about. But there may also be
other bugs in your bedroom that feed on you at night.

Bedbugs are tiny vampires. These small, brown
flattened insects are big enough to see, but they stay
well hidden. During the day they hide either under
the mattress or in cracks and crevices around the
room. At night they creep into your bed, and take a
meal of blood while you sleep.

Built for bloodsucking

Bedbugs are well adapted
for their bloodsucking
lifestyle. Their flattened
bodies make it easy for
them to squeeze into tiny
cracks and gaps where they
can hide during the day.

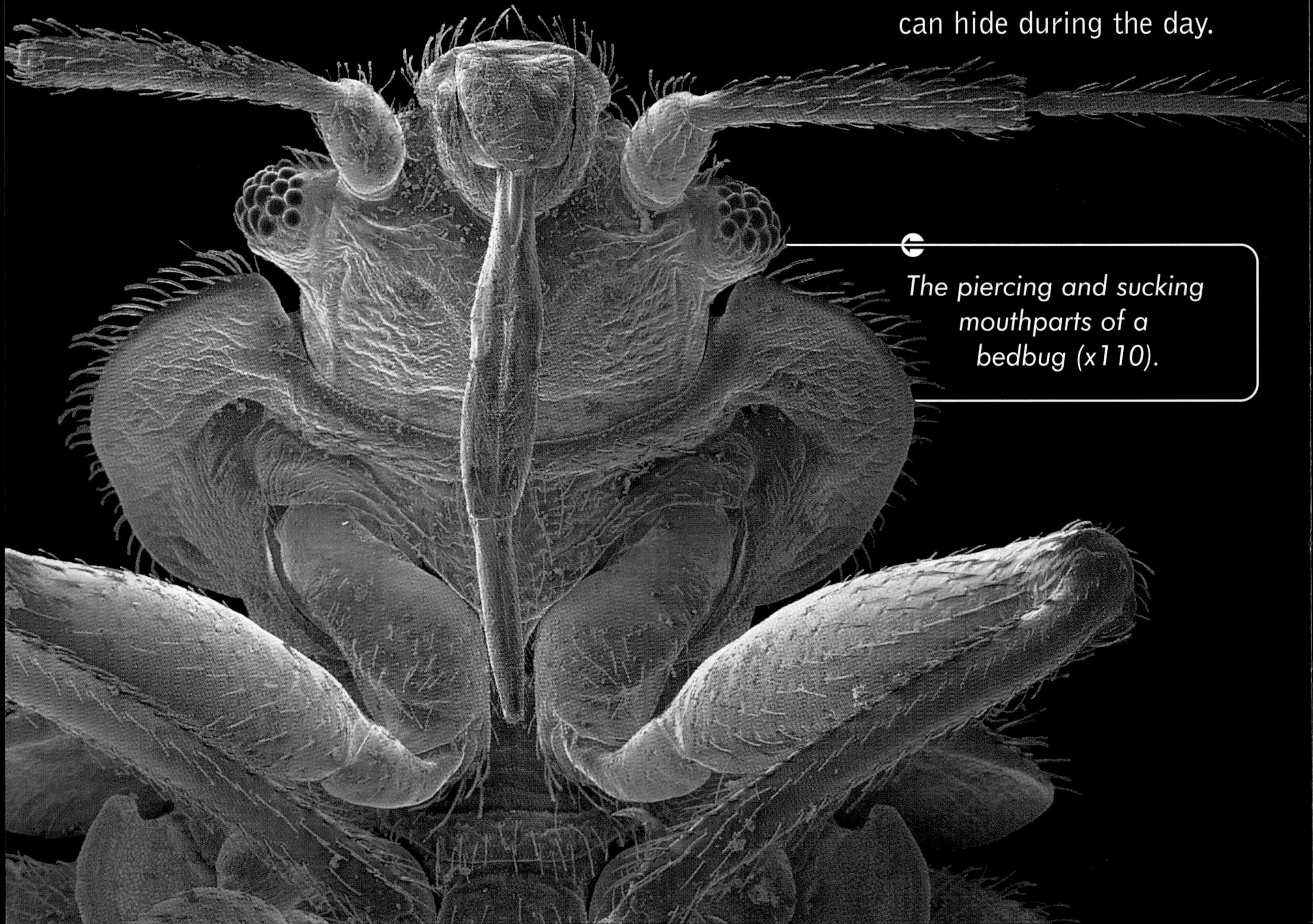

*The piercing and sucking
mouthparts of a
bedbug (x110).*

Bedbugs use their needle-like **mouthparts** to pierce human skin. Before beginning to suck blood, the bug injects saliva (spit) into the wound. Chemicals in the saliva keep the blood flowing while the bug is feeding. Soon the bedbug is completely full of blood, and crawls away to digest its meal.

People rarely wake when they are bitten by bedbugs, but the next day they have sore, itchy bites.

From egg to adult

A female bedbug can lay about 200 eggs, in the mattress or in cracks and crevices. Eggs take from 1 to 4 weeks to hatch, depending on the temperature. The **nymphs** that hatch from the eggs

Bedbugs feeding on human skin.

look like the adults, except that they are much smaller and white. A nymph **moults** five times before it becomes an adult, and it must eat at least one blood meal between each moult.

Preventing bedbugs

Bedbugs were a common pest until the middle of the 20th century, but they are much less common today. If you change your sheets regularly and vacuum your bedroom, bedbugs are unlikely to be a problem.

It is often possible to sleep soundly while bedbugs feed on you at night.

More bloodsuckers

Bedbugs aren't the only bloodsucking insects that can be found in bedrooms. If you have pets in the house, there may be fleas in the carpet.

Fleas are bloodsucking insects 2–3 millimeters long. There are many different kinds, each of which prefers to feed on a particular kind of animal. The flea most likely to find its way into your bedroom is the cat flea. These fleas live on cats and dogs, but will also suck blood from a human, leaving a sore, itchy bite.

Human fleas (x60) can jump about 70 times their height and 100 times their length. If you could do this, you would be able to jump over a block of flats!

What fleas are like

Fleas are wingless, brown insects with a small head. They are thin rather than flat, to help them slip between the hairs or feathers on an animal's body.

A flea has no wings, but it has an amazing jump. A flea's jumping ability helps it to move about in search of a **host** and to hitch a ride on a passing animal.

Eggs and young

You are more likely to find adult fleas on your pet than in the carpet, but pets that have fleas shed eggs wherever they go. Flea eggs in the carpet take between 2 and 12 days to hatch into worm-like **larvae**. The larvae find enough bits of food in the carpet to survive and grow. After two **moults**, they spin **cocoons**.

A flea can stay in its cocoon for up to a year. While inside the cocoon it cannot be killed by **pesticides**, which is why it is often difficult to get rid of fleas. When conditions are good, an adult flea emerges from the cocoon.

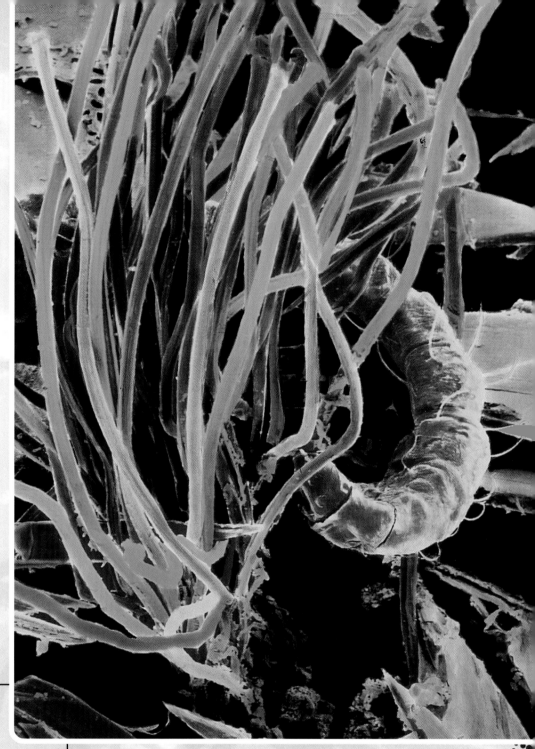

Cat flea larva coiled around the fibres in a carpet.

PEOPLE FLEAS

Another kind of flea is specialized for living on humans. These human fleas are quite rare nowadays, because they prefer to live on unwashed bodies and hide in dirty clothing. The best place to find human fleas today is in a pigsty! Pigs have a similar biology to humans, and pigsties sometimes get infested with these fleas.

Carpet crawlers

Is there a trunk of old clothes in your bedroom? Do you have a cupboard or closet with old clothes in it? These are the sorts of places you will find carpet beetle **larvae**. These hairy creatures feed on things like carpets, woollens and furniture coverings.

A carpet beetle larva tunnelling its way through a carpet.

Carpet beetles are common, but unless you get a large **infestation** you won't know they are there. Adult carpet beetles are small, rounded beetles about 2–5 millimetres long. They are often black, but sometimes they have orange or yellow patterning. The larvae are carrot-shaped and covered in bristles, with a tuft of especially long bristles on the tail.

Pollen feeders

Adult carpet beetles don't live in houses at all. They live outside and feed on flower **pollen**.

When a female carpet beetle has **mated**, she looks for somewhere to lay her eggs. Some carpet beetles

① *Head of a carpet beetle larva (x240) showing its hairy appearance.*

lay their eggs in the nests of birds, small animals or insects. However, some find their way into houses, and lay their eggs there. One female can lay up to 100 eggs.

Adult carpet beetles like the light, but their larvae prefer dark places. They feed and rest under furniture, in dark corners or in folds in cloth. Larvae prefer products made from animals, such as wool carpets, fur or hairs, but they will also eat cotton.

Larvae grow quite slowly; in warm places they take several months to reach full size, but in cooler conditions they can take as long as 3 years. Once the larva is fully grown, it forms a hard case around itself and becomes a **pupa**. When the adult beetle hatches from the pupa, it flies out of the house.

Keeping carpet beetles out

If you vacuum your bedroom regularly, making sure to do all round the edges and under the furniture, you are unlikely to get carpet beetle larvae. If you have a cupboard or chest where you store clothes, make sure they are clean before you put them away.

Clothes moths

If something is a bit battered and worse for wear, people sometimes say it looks 'moth-eaten'. Clothes moths are not as common as they were in the past, but they still occasionally invade people's homes and eat holes in their clothes.

A case-making clothes moth caterpillar. Only the head end of the caterpillar sticks out of its case.

Adult clothes moths on a jumper. Female moths rarely fly, but scuttle around instead.

If you notice tiny holes in your clothes, and white threads on the surface, then you may have clothes moths. They are very small, dull-coloured moths that live in dark, enclosed places such as wardrobes or storage chests. Adult clothes moths do not eat at all – they only live long enough to **mate** and lay eggs. But their caterpillars eat clothing, paper, fur and other materials.

Silk webs and cases

There are two kinds of clothes moth, and their caterpillars live differently. One kind spins mats or tunnels of silk as they move about. These mats may incorporate caterpillar droppings, so they make clothes messy.

The other kind of caterpillar spins itself a silk case. When it is eating or moving, the front part of the caterpillar sticks out of the case. This case-making caterpillar eats neat, round holes in clothes.

Hatching out

Female clothes moths lay up to 150 eggs, which take between 4 days and 3 weeks to hatch. The **larvae** feed until they are fully grown, then they become **pupae**. The case-making kind of caterpillar turns its silk case into a hard **cocoon**. Inside the cocoon the caterpillar turns into an adult moth.

Mothballing clothes

The best way to avoid clothes moths is to clean clothes before storing them, and to put them in airtight containers. Dried lavender, cloves, lemon peels and cedar chips are all aromatic (smelly) items that can be put into cupboards and chests where clothes are stored to keep clothing moths away. Mothballs are small balls made of pest-repellants that are designed to keep off moths. But they can damage some clothing, and clothes that have been stored with mothballs need airing or cleaning before they can be worn.

🔎 *If you store your clean clothes carefully in a dry, airtight wardrobe you can avoid getting clothes moths.*

Chewing old wood

Eating old clothes and fur is bad enough, but many kinds of insect **larvae** eat wood! If you have an old house with wooden beams, or any old furniture in your bedroom, it might have woodworm. Woodworms are the larvae of certain kinds of beetle. They spend years eating tunnels through pieces of wood, then eventually emerge into the light to live for a brief time as adults.

Furniture beetles

The most common types of woodworm are the larvae of furniture beetles. Adult furniture beetles appear in spring and early summer. They fly around looking for a **mate**. After mating, the female lays about 30 eggs in holes or cracks in wood. As soon as the larvae emerge from the eggs, they begin to burrow into the wood. They live in the wood for several years, slowly growing bigger.

When the larvae are fully grown, they work their way back to the surface of the wood. Just below the surface, each larva digs out a small chamber where it turns into a **pupa**. After a few weeks, a new adult beetle emerges from the pupa, bites its way out of the wood and flies away.

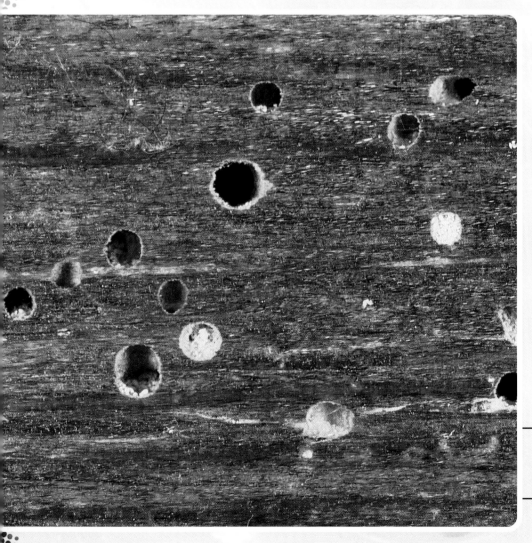

Tunnels made by woodworm can seriously weaken wood.

The death-watch beetle is bigger than the furniture beetle, and it cannot fly.

Death-watch beetles

Another kind of woodworm, found particularly in Britain, is known as the death-watch beetle. Death-watch beetles are often found in old churches. When a beetle is looking for a mate, it sends out a signal by tapping on the wood with its head. It is this tapping that gives the death-watch beetle its name. In the past, people hearing the tapping thought it was the tapping of Death coming to claim a victim!

Wood-eating termites.

TROPICAL TERRORS

In tropical countries, the biggest pest of wood is the termite. Millions of termites live together in large nests. Wood is their main food, and if they get into the roof beams of a building they can destroy them in a short time. Metal plates are sometimes fitted round the skirting boards of houses to stop termites climbing into the roof.

Mouldy and rotten

Do you sometimes take a banana to your bedroom and then forget to throw away the peel? Or perhaps you occasionally find an old apple core under the bed? Old banana peel goes black and mouldy, while apple cores go brown and rotten. Both the mould and the rot are caused by **fungi**.

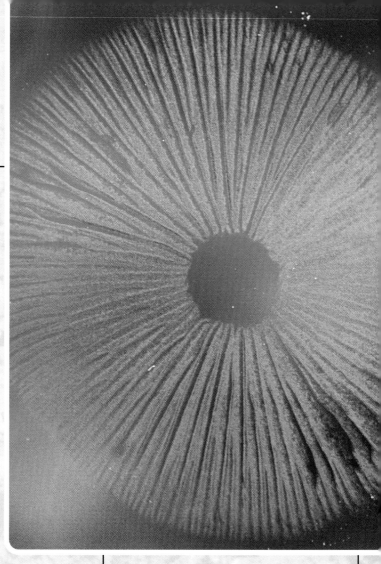

The spores of a mushroom are on the gills that cover the underside of the cap. If you leave the cap of a mushroom on a piece of paper overnight, you get a spore print like this when the spores fall from the gills.

The brown lumps on this apple are caused by the fungus Penicillium.

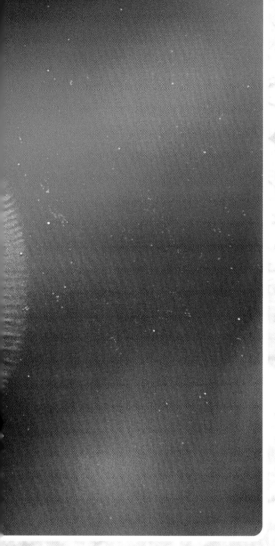

other fruits are also made up of masses of hyphae. These tiny fungal threads invade the fruit. A fungus has no mouth or **digestive system** – it has to simply absorb its food. To get food from the fruit, it releases chemicals that break it down into simple **nutrients** that the fungus can absorb. It is these chemicals that cause the flesh of a rotting apple to turn almost liquid.

Producing spores

Once a mould has begun to grow and spread, it produces millions of powdery spores. The spores are the seeds that will allow the fungus to spread and grow elsewhere. Bunches of spores grow on tiny stalks, and as they ripen they are released into the air. The spores are light enough to be carried by the slightest current of air.

Releasing poisons

When an apple goes rotten, it's quite easy to scrape off the rotten part and eat the rest. But eating mouldy food isn't a good idea. As well as the chemicals they release to digest their food, many moulds produce toxins (poisons). These toxins can spread through the fruit, beyond the area of the mould growth, and make you very ill.

A magnified view (x1210) of the tiny spores of the Penicillium *fungus.*

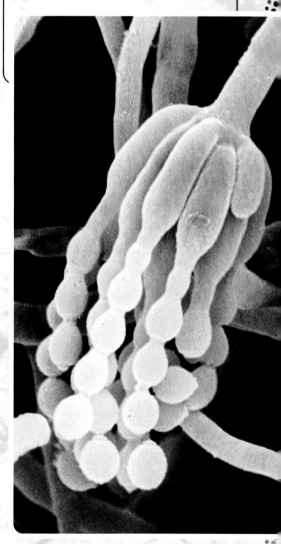

The best known types of fungi are mushrooms and toadstools. But what we call mushrooms are not the main mushroom fungus at all – they are structures for producing fungal **spores** (seeds). The 'body' of the mushroom fungus is a mass of incredibly thin threads called **hyphae**, which grow hidden beneath the ground.

Invading threads

The mould fungi that grow on apples, bananas and

Passengers and parasites

Woodworms, clothes moths, carpet beetles and many other kinds of insect often have their own, even smaller passengers. They are mites, relatives of the dust mites that live in the carpet. Some kinds are hitch-hikers that use insects as air transport. Others are **scavengers** or **parasites**.

Tiny hitch-hikers

Any insects that get into your bedroom are likely to be carrying tiny mite hitch-hikers with them. Mites cannot fly, so when for instance some young plant-eating mites want to get away from their home plant, they hitch a ride.

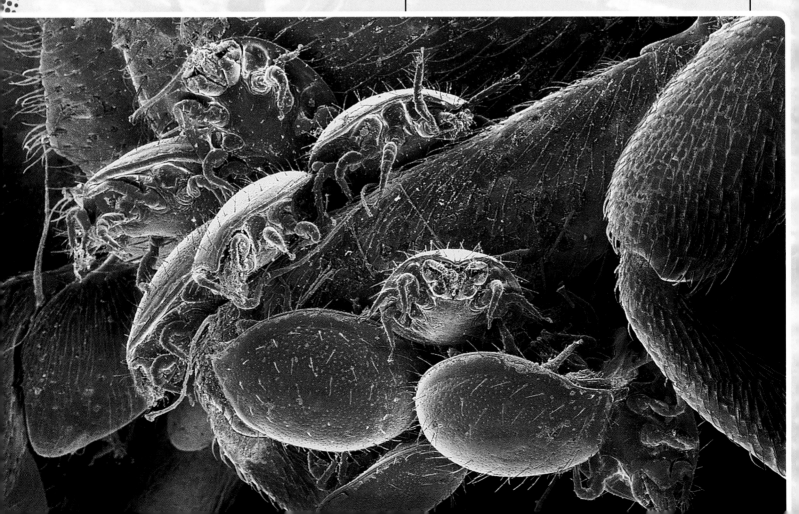

Mites hitching a ride on the legs of a beetle (x64).

Scavenger mites

Some mites spend most of their time on a particular type of insect, but they do not feed on the insect. Instead they are scavengers, eating up bits of food that the insect leaves behind, or feeding on **fungi** that live in the insect's nest. Beetles are often the **hosts** of scavenger mites.

Parasites

Woodworms would seem to have an easy life, protected from **predators** and with a plentiful food supply. But they do have enemies – parasitic mites. These mites live on the woodworm and feed on its body. Because woodworms take so long to grow, there is time for the mites to reproduce, and often mite numbers become so great that they kill their host.

There are many different parasitic mites found on insects. Two of the best known are parasites of honey bees. One very tiny

A grain mite feeding on fungus. Fungus-feeding mites often carry their own hitch-hikers: pieces of fungus or fungal **spores**.

kind called *Acarapis woodi* lives its whole life in a honey bee's breathing tubes. At first these mites do not greatly bother the bee, but heavy mite **infestations** can weaken or kill a whole bee **colony**.

The other honey bee mite is the *Varroa* mite. This is bigger and lives on the outside of the bee. *Varroa* mites often kill their hosts. In recent years, *Varroa* mites that are **resistant** to **pesticides** have become a huge problem for beekeepers everywhere.

Varroa *mite on a honey bee (x74).*

Table of sizes

Although all hidden life is tiny, there is a huge range of sizes. To a flea, a grain of pollen seems just as tiny as the flea seems to us!

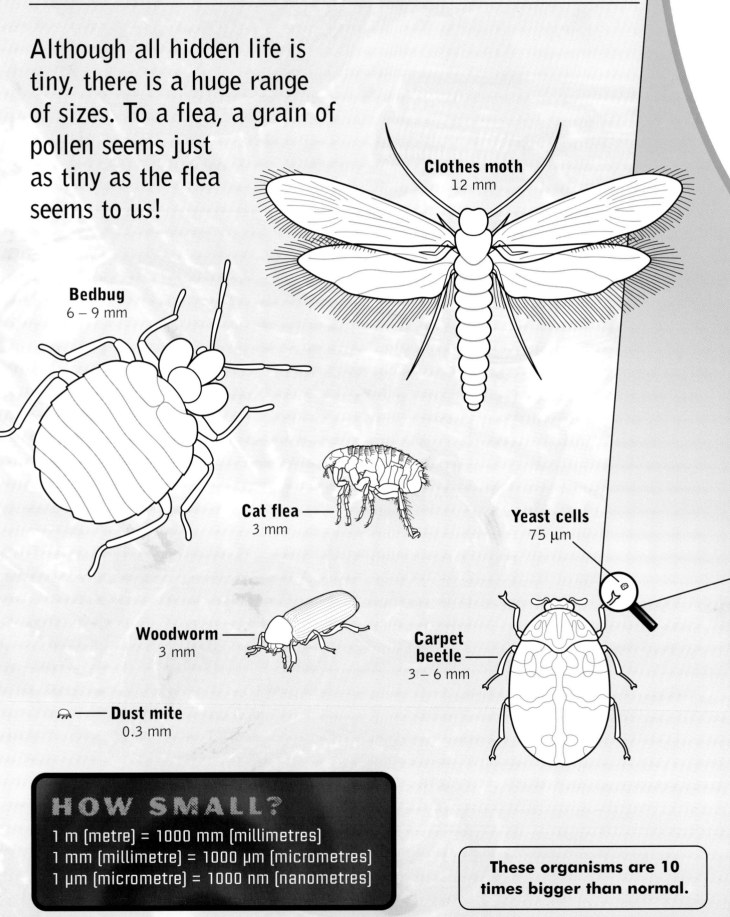

Clothes moth
12 mm

Bedbug
6 – 9 mm

Cat flea
3 mm

Yeast cells
75 µm

Woodworm
3 mm

Carpet beetle
3 – 6 mm

Dust mite
0.3 mm

HOW SMALL?

1 m (metre) = 1000 mm (millimetres)
1 mm (millimetre) = 1000 µm (micrometres)
1 µm (micrometre) = 1000 nm (nanometres)

These organisms are **10 times bigger than normal.**

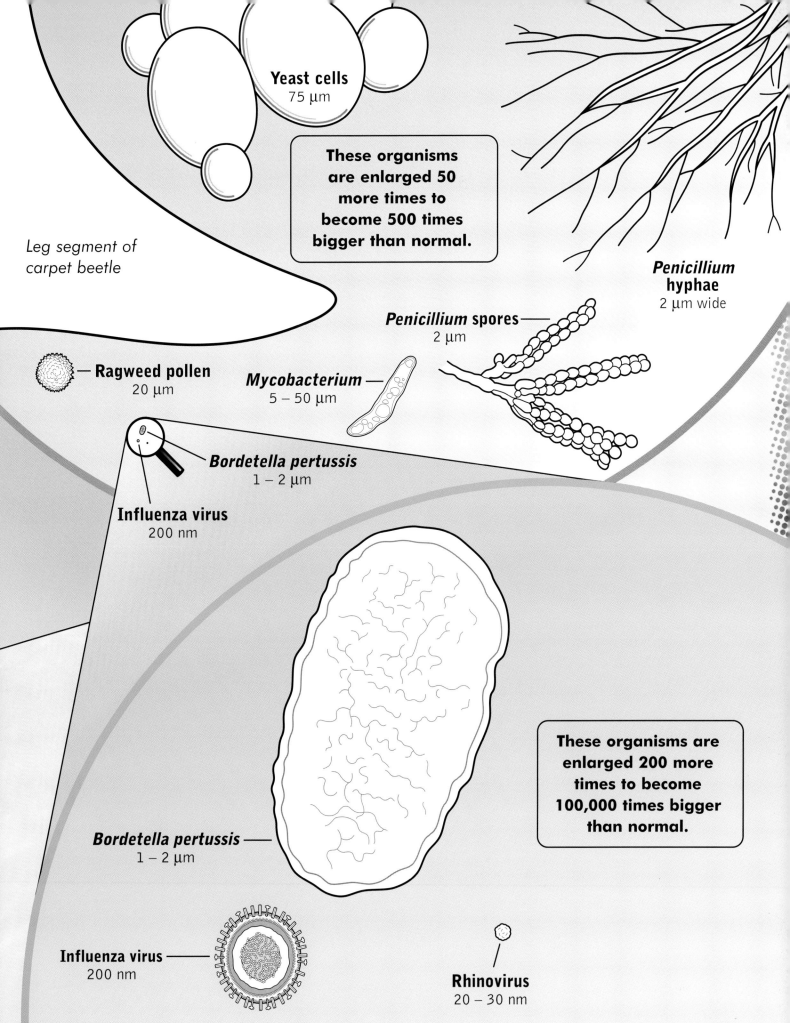

Yeast cells
75 μm

These organisms are enlarged 50 more times to become 500 times bigger than normal.

Penicillium hyphae
2 μm wide

Leg segment of carpet beetle

Penicillium spores
2 μm

Ragweed pollen
20 μm

Mycobacterium
5 – 50 μm

Bordetella pertussis
1 – 2 μm

Influenza virus
200 nm

These organisms are enlarged 200 more times to become 100,000 times bigger than normal.

Bordetella pertussis
1 – 2 μm

Influenza virus
200 nm

Rhinovirus
20 – 30 nm

29

Glossary

airborne carried in the air

allergic when the body overreacts to something that you breathe in or eat or get on your skin. It can cause sneezing, or a rash, or a sickness such as asthma.

asthma disease of the lungs that causes wheezing and other breathing difficulties

atmosphere the air around us

bacteria (singular – bacterium) very tiny creatures, each one only a single cell. They are different from other single-celled creatures because they don't have a nucleus.

cells building blocks of living things. Some living things are just single cells, others are made up of billions of cells working together.

climate type of weather a region normally has

cocoon silky, cigar-shaped case spun by many insect larvae to protect them while they change from larvae into adults

colony group of creatures of one kind living close together

digestive system stomach, intestines and other parts of the animal that break down food into nutrients that the body can absorb and use for energy

DNA material that makes up the genes of living cells

electron microscope very powerful microscope that can magnify objects up to half a million times

fungi (singular – fungus) plant-like living things such as mushrooms and yeasts

host animal or plant that a parasite lives on

hyphae thin, thread-like cells that make up the body of most fungi

infestation when something is overrun with a harmful or irritating creature such as an insect

larvae (singular – larva) young stage of some types of creatures. Larvae look different from adults, and may have to go through a changing stage in order to become adults.

mate when a male and female animal get together to reproduce

microbe microscopic creature such as bacteria and viruses

moult to shed skin, feathers or hair

mouthparts jaws or other parts that an insect uses to take in food

nucleus round structure surrounded by a membrane, found inside a living cell. It contains the cell's genes.

nutrients chemicals that nourish living things

nymph the young of some types of creatures. Nymphs usually look similar to their parents, and change gradually into adults over several months.

parasite creature that lives on or in another living creature and takes its food from it, without giving any benefit in return

pesticide chemical that is used to kill insects or other animals that are pests, for instance those that cause disease or eat crops

pollen fine powder produced by flowers. If pollen is carried by wind or insects to other flowers of the same kind, it fertilizes them.

predator animal that hunts and kills other animals for food

pupa (plural – pupae) a stage in the growth of an insect in which the insect changes from a larva into an adult

resistance body's ability to fight off disease

scavenger animal that feeds on dead or waste material

spores fungal spores are like very tiny fungal 'seeds'. Bacterial spores are bacteria that have formed a tough outer coat to help them survive difficult conditions.

vaccinate to inject someone with vaccine. Vaccine is a substance that protects you from getting a particular disease by stimulating your body's defences against that disease.

viruses extremely tiny microbes that cannot grow or reproduce by themselves, but have to infect a living cell to do so

Further reading

Cells and Life: The Diversity of Life, Robert Snedden, (Heinemann Library, 2002)

Cells and Life: The World of the Cell, Robert Snedden, (Heinemann Library, 2002)

DK Mega Bites: Microlife: The Microscopic World of Tiny Creatures, David Burnie, (Dorling Kindersley, 2002)

Horrible Science: Microscopic Monsters, Nick Arnold (illustrated by Tony de Saulles), (Barbour Books, 2001)

Microlife: A World of Microorganisms, Robert Snedden, (Heinemann Library, 2000)

Websites

Cells Alive! (www.cellsalive.com)
Pictures, videos and interactive pages about cells and microbes. The How Big? page shows the sizes of creatures from mites to viruses.

Virtual Microscopy (www.micro.magnet.fsu.edu/primer/virtual/virtual.html)
On this interactive website you can pick from a selection of samples, adjust the focus, change the magnification, and use a whole range of powerful microscopes.

Microbe Zoo (www.commtechlab.msu.edu/sites/dlc-me/zoo/)
A site about strange microbes.

Microbe World (www.microbeworld.org/home.htm)
Information, pictures, movies and activities exploring the world of microbes.

The Mighty Mites (www.earthlife.net/chelicerata/acari.html)
A simple and fun introduction to mites, including links to other mite sites.

Index